# Historic Hilton Trust

# The Stones of the Pictish Peninsulas of Easter Ross and the Black Isle

by

©Douglas Scott

for

The Historic Hilton Trust

May 2004

Published By
Historic Hilton Trust

# Introduction

Dougie Scott's booklet provides a very welcome guide to the Pictish stones and heritage of Ross-shire for both visitors and locals alike.

It will give everyone who wishes to explore the Pictish Trail a handy pocket-sized guide to take with them, giving a flavour of the Pictish culture that dominated life in the Fearn Peninsula and surrounding area over a thousand years ago.

The Historic Hilton Trust, who commissioned Dougie Scott to produce this booklet, are one of a number of local trusts who aim to promote and preserve the Pictish heritage in Easter Ross and the Black Isle. I very much hope they will all help to make this informative booklet widely available.

Richard Durham
*Chairman*
*Historic Hilton Trust*

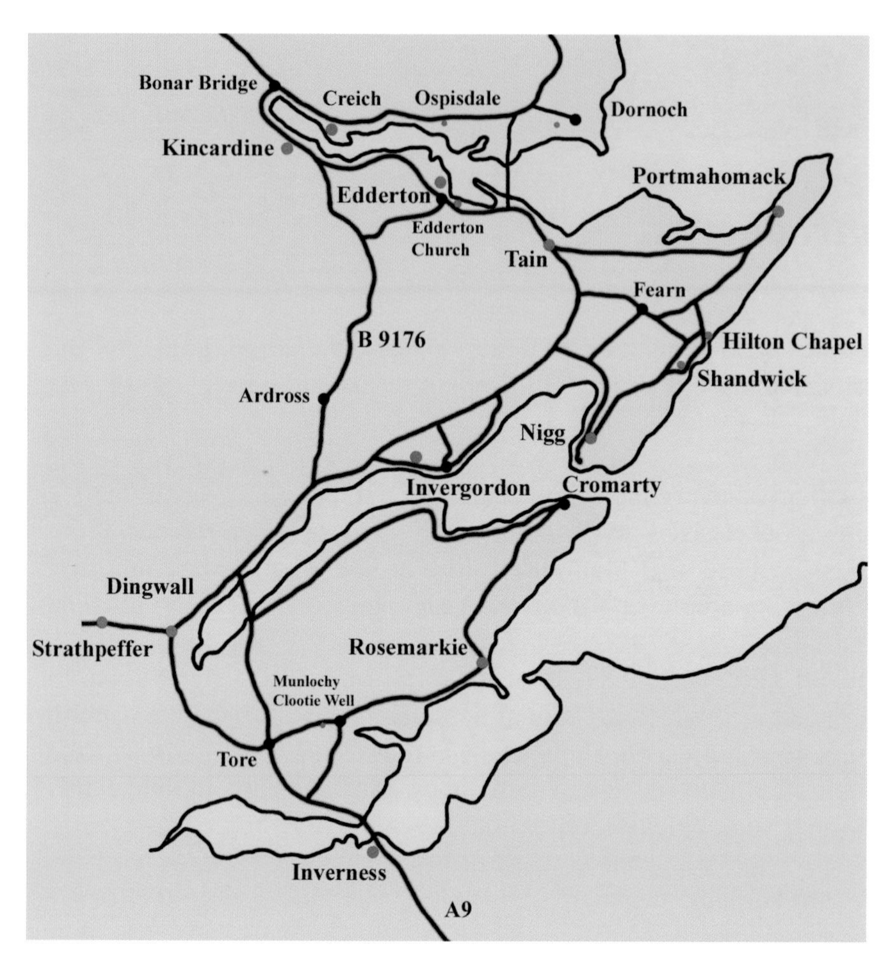


A map of the Fearn and Tarbat Peninsulas, Easter Ross and the Black Isle with the locations of the Pictish symbol and bronze age stones shown in red.

## The Edderton Stone

In the area of the Dornoch and Cromarty Firths, there are a number of prehistoric stones carved with Pictish symbols. One of the more interesting of these, stands near the remains of a bronze age stone circle in the village of Edderton. The symbols are of a salmon leaping over a vertically placed double disc and Z rod. I first went to Edderton with Iain Frazer, a friend who lived in the village and he told me the standing stone once stood at the centre of a large mound. According to a local legend, this was where a Viking leader had been buried after being killed in a battle against the Scots. Even though the stone and circle are at least 4000 years old, because these symbols are dated from about the 5$^{th}$ to the 7$^{th}$ century AD, it's more likely this had been a Pictish, rather than a Viking burial mound. Pictish symbols come in different forms and combinations and are thought to represent family crests. The double discs on the stone have inner concentric circles with the lower disc having a smaller circle displaced to its top. Closer examination of the lower disc also revealed a small artificial hole to the top of the inner disc.

This is the first of four holes placed around the eastern side of the stone in a line that ends with a large deep hole at the centre of its southern side. To the upper right of this is a faint horizontal line of what might be a form of ancient writing called Ogham.

All that remains of the circle is an arc of five small stones and a central burial cist, which was found when the Rev. J.M. Joass excavated the site in 1866. The burial cist contained a beaker packed with charcoal, burnt bone and a few teeth. The remains of this beaker can be seen along with many other Pictish symbol stones in the museum at Dunrobin castle. As it's partially surrounded by a wide ditch on its northern side, the site may also be a type of monument called a henge. One of the most striking things about the two stones forming the open end of the circle is that they are in line with the standing stone, which is pointing southwest towards the hill of Tor Leathan. In 1903 Romilly Allen and Joseph Anderson mentioned the alignment in their definitive work on Pictish art the "Early Christian Monuments of Scotland". They also speculated about the difference between the age of the stones and the Pictish carvings and commented the stone was known locally as the Clach Biorach, the pointed stone.

I also knew these outlying stones pointed to where the sun or moon would rise or set along the horizon at certain specific times. So with the help of another friend, Terry Kelly, we surveyed the line of the Clach Biorach from the circle and found it was pointing to where the sun set on Tor Leathan on the 5 November - 4 February. These two dates are roughly the same time of year celebrated by the later Celts as the festivals of Samhain, (Sowain) and Bride. Samhain in early November is the same festival we now call Halloween or bonfire night. These festivals occurred about 45 days before and after midwinter and Samhain is the time in Celtic folklore when the spirits of the ancestors can cross back into the world to haunt the living. This apparently is what children represent when guising on the night of Halloween.

The Pictish symbols on the north side of the Clach Biorach comprise of a salmon and a double disc and Z rod. From the stone circle below, the Clach Biorach points to where the sun will set on the 5th November and as the image below shows on the 4th February 2003.

The aerial photograph shows the position of the Dounie stone to the upper centre of the picture.

There used to be another large stone standing near the farm of Dounie some two kilometres to the northwest of Edderton. Although it is now lying about 50m to the north of its original site at that point we didn't know the stone's exact location as it was moved in the early 1970's. It was then quite by chance that Margaret Urquhart, a teacher at Tain academy, on hearing of our interest, gave us an aerial photograph of the Dounie stone taken in 1959. Even though this picture had been taken from 29000 ft, it was possible to see the faint smudge and the shadow cast by the stone. By comparing certain features from the photograph, we managed by survey to locate the position of this stone to within a few metres. Leaving Terry at the stone's original position I went back to the Clach Biorach and saw that even from 2 km he was easily visible and was standing directly beneath a notch on the northwest horizon. A survey of the notch revealed this was where the upper edge of the midsummer sun would have set some four thousand years ago.

Due to changes in the Earth's axis the midsummer sun now sets to the south of the notch, but 4000 years from the standing stone ago the upper edge of the midsummer sun would have set in the notch.

When we surveyed the notch from the circle we were astounded to find that the lower edge of the sun would have set into this feature. This means the distance between the circle and the Clach Biorach was the same as the sun's observed diameter on the ground and would have enabled the builders to determine the exact day of the summer solstice. As these two outlying stones were pointing to where the sun set at different times of the year, it seems likely this was connected in some ritualistic way to the burial in the circle. At the southern end of the Struie ridge, another distinctive notch on the horizon was where the sun would set at the times of equal day and night called the equinoxes on the 21 March- 21 September. The equinoxes are the times of year when the sun is halfway between midsummer and midwinter. The top of Struie hill is where the sun sets 45 days before and after midsummer on the 4th of May and 7th of August and these are the same times as the Celtic festivals of Beltane and Lughnasa.

As the sun was photographed setting on the top of Struie Hill on the 4 May - 7 August 1989, this means the hill could have been used to mark the festivals at Beltane and Lughnasa. The picture below shows the autumn equinox sun setting in the Struie notch on the 21/ 9 / 02.

Even though these two horizon features were not indicated in any way we felt that, as the other sunset positions were marked and the Beltane and equinox orientations are found at other sites, it seems obvious the people here would also have known about them.

During the bronze age, the position of the circle could only have been found by someone deliberately watching where the sun set on hilltops and notches about every 45 days on the western horizon throughout the year. The only solar position that wasn't marked was where the winter solstice sun would have set on the flat southwest horizon. Was the circle originally built for some high-ranking individual, or was the burial used to make the site sacred? As we have only a little of the archaeological information, this cannot be answered with any certainty. Later research suggests the double disc symbols evolved from bronze age rock carvings called cupmarks and represent the midwinter and midsummer sun, while the two crescents, the first and last phase of the moon during the month. As Halloween is still celebrated today means it's likely the Picts knew the Clach Biorach marked the festival of Samhain and carved their sacred ancestral symbols on the stone perhaps to honour someone who may still lie buried nearby.

Although we will never fully understand what the stones had been used for, from experience I can guarantee the sun will set along the western horizon as described from the stones at Edderton. I particularly remember a few days after the partial eclipse of the sun on 30th May 1984 at 1:20 on the 3rd of June, standing by the Clach Biorach watching as the lower edge of the three day old moon set perfectly in the midsummer notch. The sky that night was cut by the quick flashes of meteorites and I could see the pale blue-green glimmer of reflected earthlight on the darkened side of the slim crescent moon. In the warm quiet of the night as the moon slid silently out of sight I was deeply moved by the simple beauty of the event. Even now after many years of surveying standing stones and cairns throughout Scotland, in my experience, no other ancient monument comes close to the sophistication of Edderton.

**Edderton Church**

About a kilometre to the east of the stone circle, at Edderton church, there is a 9th to 10th century AD Pictish cross slab. This stone has on its west side a large Celtic cross, while the other side has two partially buried Pictish warriors on horseback with another rider above. It's recently been found the lower part of the cross is formed by Calvary steps. In 1992 Richard Easson and myself found, among the broken gravestones in the ruins of the small chapel at the east end of the church, the fragments of another two cross slabs. These cross slabs were found in 1903 just after the publication of Allen and Anderson's book, but while being photographed and published by the minister, the Rev. Macrae, they had apparently been forgotten and were later broken up. Richard did some research and found that not only was the Rev. Macrae's daughter living at Nigg, she still had her fathers notebooks. Apparently the Rev. Macrae had been a keen antiquarian and had found in the 14th century medieval Scotichronicon, that the monks at Edderton had to move to Nova Farina near the village of Fearn in 1227 due to the increasing ferocity of clan warfare.

## The Edderton Cross Slab

When the stone was raised for conservation in early May, 2004, it was found the bottom of the cross was carved with a stepped Calvary base.

Another enigmatic Pictish stone from Ardjachie near Tain is carved with a number of cupmarks surrounding a rayed sun disc, and a rare right angle symbol. While sun discs are found with bronze age cupmarks, these last two symbols are also found on the Pictish stones at Knockando and from Ardross. The Ardross Stone can be seen with others from the same area in Inverness Museum.

As the sun disc on the Ardjachie Stone is surrounded by cupmarks, it's obvious this would have been carved first. This creates a problem as the early Pictish symbols have been dated from the $5^{th}$ to $7^{th}$ century AD, whereas the cupmarks were made 4000 years ago during the bronze age. While the Pictish double disc symbols seem to have evolved from bronze age cup and ringmarks, there are recent accounts of people in the highlands turning small stones or pouring milk in cupmarks in order to thank supernatural beings called the Sidhe (Shee) and a female deity called the Gruagaich for the continued fertility of the land and for protecting the cattle from harm. This is perhaps why cupmarks in Gaelic are called Clach Aoraidh, Clach Orach, the wishing or praying stones. This however, is probably a continuity of an ancient tradition, rather than the creation of new cupmarks, so the problem of the date of the Ardjachie Stone still remains a mystery. The Sidhe were believed to live in cairns and standing stones and it's likely they are a faint racial memory of the spirits of the people who were buried in the cairns. It is suggested this contact was made when the sun or moon rose or set in line with the cupmarked stones at times like Samhain or midwinter. The Ardjachie Stone and the remains of the Edderton cross slabs can be seen at Tain Through Time.

At Kincardine Church there is a coffin shaped stone with some worn images of horsemen, while on the other side of the Dornoch Firth, next to the graveyard at Creich, is St Demhan's Cross Slab. To the east at Ospisdale there is a tall stone standing next to the road, which like the Clach Biorach also has a large deep hole on its southern side. About a kilometre west of Dornoch at Drumdriven there is a standing stone with a cupmark on its western side.

The Ardjachie Stone, Tain

## Tarbat Church

Around the coasts of the Fearn and Tarbat Peninsulas are the locations of a number of Christian Pictish cross slabs of the 8$^{th}$ to 9$^{th}$ century AD. These cross slabs are a combination of Irish Christian and early Pictish art, with one side expressing the new belief, while the other shows displays of local power. Fragments of these stones have been found over the years at the church at Tarbat, Portmahomack. Excavations by Prof. Martin Carver of York University from the early 1990's to the present day have shown the area around the church formed an important monastic settlement about the same time as the founding of Iona by St Columba in 563 AD. Apart from other fragments of Pictish carved stones, the excavations also found an industrial area where bronze and silver were worked. Other finds suggested they had been used in the making of vellum and illuminated manuscripts similar to the Book of Kells or the Lindisfarne Gospels. Further evidence suggests the monastery was burnt to the ground during a Viking raid. The results of the excavation are on show in the church along with fragments of cross slabs by the Tarbat Historic Trust.

**The Dragon or Apostle Stone, Tarbat**

## St Mary's Chapel, Hilton

In the village of Hilton, is the ruin of the St Mary's chapel where one of the most magnificent Pictish cross slabs was located. The Hilton Stone used to stand at the chapel's western end until 1676 when it was cut down and its cross side destroyed and reused by a farmer as a gravestone. However, the stone was too heavy and it wasn't moved until it was taken to Invergordon castle in 1884. When fire destroyed the castle in 1921, the stone was given to the British Museum in London. This caused such anger in Scotland, it was returned to Edinburgh where it can be seen in the National Museums of Scotland. Prior to the erection of a replica, when the western side of the chapel was excavated by Glasgow University's Guard Unit in 2000, thousands of fragments from the cross side of the stone were found. Under these, its broken base was also found where it had originally stood 1200 years ago. At the top of the stone there is a very faint double disc symbol, each disc carved with solar triskeles. Among the vine branches growing out of a small vase up the sides of the stone representing the 'Tree of Life' there are some birds and griffins eating the berries of salvation.

Original picture ©Tain Museum

An image of the lower part of the Hilton Stone was digitally joined with another taken at Invergordon Castle in the early 20th century, to show how one side of the stone would have originally looked.

As the base of the Hilton Stone has been buried for perhaps a thousand years, the carvings are still very sharp and in superb condition.

In the panel below there is a Crescent and V rod above two round discs of knot work. The central panel shows a hunting scene with a woman riding side-saddle next to a mirror and comb symbol. Her importance is shown as she overlays the image of her bearded 'husband' and it's likely she either commissioned or is the person to whom the stone is dedicated. The bottom panel of triple spirals has a circle at the centre, within which there are traces of what seems to have been a simple Christian cross. On the other side of the stone is the stepped base of a Christian cross with two coiled dragons on either side. Even though the cross side has been broken into thousands of fragments, Heather James and a team of people from GUARD are slowly matching these together, so we may eventually see what the cross looked like. The aim of the Hilton Trust is make sure the base stays within the local community. If you would like to help, please fill in the form at the back of this booklet where you will also find information about viewing the Hilton Stone.

## The Shandwick Stone

From Hilton follow the road south to Shandwick where another cross slab can be seen standing above the village. Local people, concerned by the erosion of the stone formed the Shandwick Trust and it is now protected from the elements in a glass box. There is a local tradition that unbaptised babies who had died during birth were buried near the stone. The seaward side of the Shandwick Stone has a worn cross, formed by 54 triple spirals. Under this there are angels, animals and coiled snakes. On its western side there are six panels. From the top there is a worn double disc symbol while below is a 'Pictish Beast' and three small animals. The next panel shows warriors on horses and a variety of creatures, including bulls, an eagle, a boar and deer. At the centre of this, is a tall figure with a monstrous open jawed head that is devouring a man while holding his leg. The horseman on the right could be thrusting at the giant with a sword or trying to rescue the man by pulling at his leg. There is also a man on a goat, and two figures fighting with swords and square shields. The largest panel is a stunning 'sunburst' of interconnecting triple spirals.

**The Shandwick Stone**

## Nigg Old Church

At the southern end of the Fearn peninsula in the church at Nigg there is a beautiful Pictish cross slab. With its delicate carvings of twisting beasts on the cross and raised bosses, this is an outstanding example of Pictish craftsmanship. The other side of the stone is very worn, but its border of superb knot work and key patterns surround a panel topped with an eagle. Under this are a Pictish beast, various animals, a harp and number of people taking part in a hunting scene. Over the years the stone has been damaged when it was blown down by storms and some parts are missing. A large fragment of the Pictish beast was recently found next to the burn below the church. This is currently on show in Tain Museum while the cross slab is inside the church under the care of the Nigg Old Trust. As the carvings on the Nigg and the other local cross slabs are similar in style to the high crosses on Iona, this could suggest a sculptural connection between the two areas. Local legend tells that the last three cross slabs mark where the bodies of Viking princes were washed ashore after their ship was wrecked on the rocks now called the King's Sons.

**The Nigg Stone**

## The Clach a' Mheirlich, Rosskeen

The Cromarty Firth has several early Pictish stones along its eastern shore. The first of these is called the Clach a' Mheirlich, Thief's Stone and stands in a field at Rosskeen, a few kilometres to the west of Invergordon. The symbols on the southern side of the stone are very worn, but night photographs show an arc symbol above a disc overlaid by a line. This might be a mirror symbol with perhaps a very faint comb symbol to its lower right. Below this is a pincer or split sword symbol and on the stone's eastern side, there is a stepped symbol. On its north side there may be a vertical double disc symbol, but this is very difficult to see even when the stone is side lit. The next stone stands just inside the gate of Dingwall's St Clements's Church. On its east side there are six cupmarks as well as three circles and a crescent and V rod. On the stone's other side, there is a double disc and Z rod above two crescent and V rods. Although it was found in the church, as the early Christian's tended to reuse earlier sacred sites, it's possible this stone was here long before any church and it seems to have retained its power from the bronze age till the Pictish period.

The Clach Mheirlich (Thief's Stone), Invergordon

Showing the east and west sides of the Pictish stone in St Clement's Church in Dingwall.

**The Eagle Stone, Strathpeffer**

From Dingwall, if you head west towards Strathpeffer you can see the Pictish Clach an Tiompain, the sounding stone, which has an arc symbol placed above that of an eagle. About halfway between the two towns you will see rising to the left, the great bronze age hillfort of Knockfarall. At some point in the past the fort was destroyed by fire, causing the surface of the stones of the fort's wall to melt and vitrify in the great heat.

The Clach an Tiompain, or the Eagle Stone as it's known today, stands near the top of the last field on your right when entering Strathpeffer. Park at the old railway station then follow the path below the 'Red House' from the main road. The stone is mentioned in the prophesies of the 16$^{th}$ century Brahn Seer, who predicted that if the stone fell three times, boats would sail up the Strath and use it as an anchor. So far the stone has fallen twice! But don't worry about global warming or melting ice caps just yet, as the Brahn Seer didn't manage to predict his own death when he was burnt in a tar barrel for witchcraft at Chanonry Point on the Black Isle.

## Groam House Museum, Rosemarkie

The Black Isle is a long peninsula and it was so named by Norse settlers because of the dark colour of the soil. Near Munlochy next to the road from Dingwall is the Clootie well, where there is a tradition if you have an ailment; you tie a cloot or rag to a tree near the well. As the cloth rots away, your health will return. This ritual can be found throughout the British Isles and dates back at least 2500 years when expensive objects of gold or bronze were offered to please the water spirits. Chanonry Point near Fortrose, where it juts out into the Moray Firth is also a good place to see dolphins. At Rosemarkie a large cross slab was found buried within the church and was erected outside where it stood for many years before being moved to Groam House Museum. Along with other beautifully carved local Pictish stones there is also information about monastic life and exhibitions showing the complexities of Celtic Art. The top part of the Rosemarkie Stone is missing and while the carvings are worn, it's still possible to see on one side, two panels of knot work, the upper of which is formed by a small squared Christian cross.

**The Rosemarkie Stone**

Along the broken top edge on the other side of the slab, the lower part of a large Crescent and V Rod symbol can be seen. Below this are another two Crescent and V Rods interspersed by a double disc symbol, while a Christian cross and key patterns occupy the lower panels. The inside of each disc of the double disc symbol on the stone is made up of seven worn triple spirals forming triskeles. This is essentially the same pattern as the other double discs found at Shandwick, Hilton, and on other Pictish stones throughout Scotland, such as at Aberlemno in Angus.

These triple spirals can be traced back through Irish art to the 5000-year-old midwinter aligned passage cairn of Newgrange and are accepted as being solar symbols. These symbols were also placed in single discs at the centre of Celtic crosses and it's likely they represent Christ himself. As there were still beliefs in solar gods throughout Europe, it looks as if the figure of Christ was introduced as the new incarnation of the sun god of everlasting life, tapping into deeply rooted traditions in order to convert people to the new belief. This would also explain why St. Patrick in his Confession compares "the worship of the sun which rises by the command of God, to the worship of the true sun which is Christ, the first leading to pain and damnation, the other to eternal life".

It therefore looks as if the Picts used one of their most sacred symbols of the life giving sun to symbolise Christ when he said, 'I am the light of the world'. While the exact meaning of early Pictish symbols is open to speculation, but when they were first carved, everyone would have understood what they meant. By combining their ancient ancestral symbols with the cross of the new faith, the Picts created one of the most outstanding forms of religious art the world has ever seen.

**The Historic Hilton Trust** would like to thank the following for their co-operation and help in producing this booklet.

The Edderton Old Church, Edderton.

Groam House Museum, High Street, Rosemarkie, IV10 8UF.
Tel: 01381 620961
groamhouse@ecosse.net

The Nigg Old Trust, Nigg
www.niggoldtrust.org.uk

The Shandwick Stone Trust, Shandwick

The Seaboard Memorial Hall, Balintore.
Tel: 01862 832888

Tain Through Time, Tower Street, Tain. IV19 1DY
Tel: 01862 894089.
info@tainmuseum.demon.co.uk
www.tainmuseum.demon.co.uk

The Tarbat Discovery Centre, Portmahomack, IV20 1YA
Tel: 01862 871351
info@tarbat-discovery.co.uk
www.tarbat-discovery.co.uk

Douglas Scott, Tain Silver, 2 Bank Street, Tain
Tel: 01862 894297
douglas.scottt@virgin.net

I would personally like to thank Liz Whiteford whose energy and enthusiasm ensured the production of this booklet.

For further information about viewing the base of the Hilton Stone contact the Seaboard Memorial Hall on 01862 832888.

**This project is part funded by:** ***Awards for All Scotland*** and the ***EU Highlands & Islands Special Transitional Programme.***

# Historic Hilton Trust

Membership Form

Name ________________________________________

Address ________________________________________

________________________________________

Signature __________________________ Date_________

I wish to be a member of the Historic Hilton Trust and enclose the sum of £3.00 annual subscription fee.

Please return to:

Historic Hilton Trust
c/o Seaboard Memorial Hall
Balintore
Ross-shire
IV20 1UA

**Thank you for your support**